Joseph Fleming
colorblind
photography

Being colorblind gives an advantage when composing black & white... less confusion. This special collection selected from thousands of captures. All images were framed in the camera and presented without edits, genuine as seen through the lens. Panchromatic conversion applied by unique proprietary process.
Original fine art and custom work available.

info@ BEACHNOISE.com

Joseph Fleming

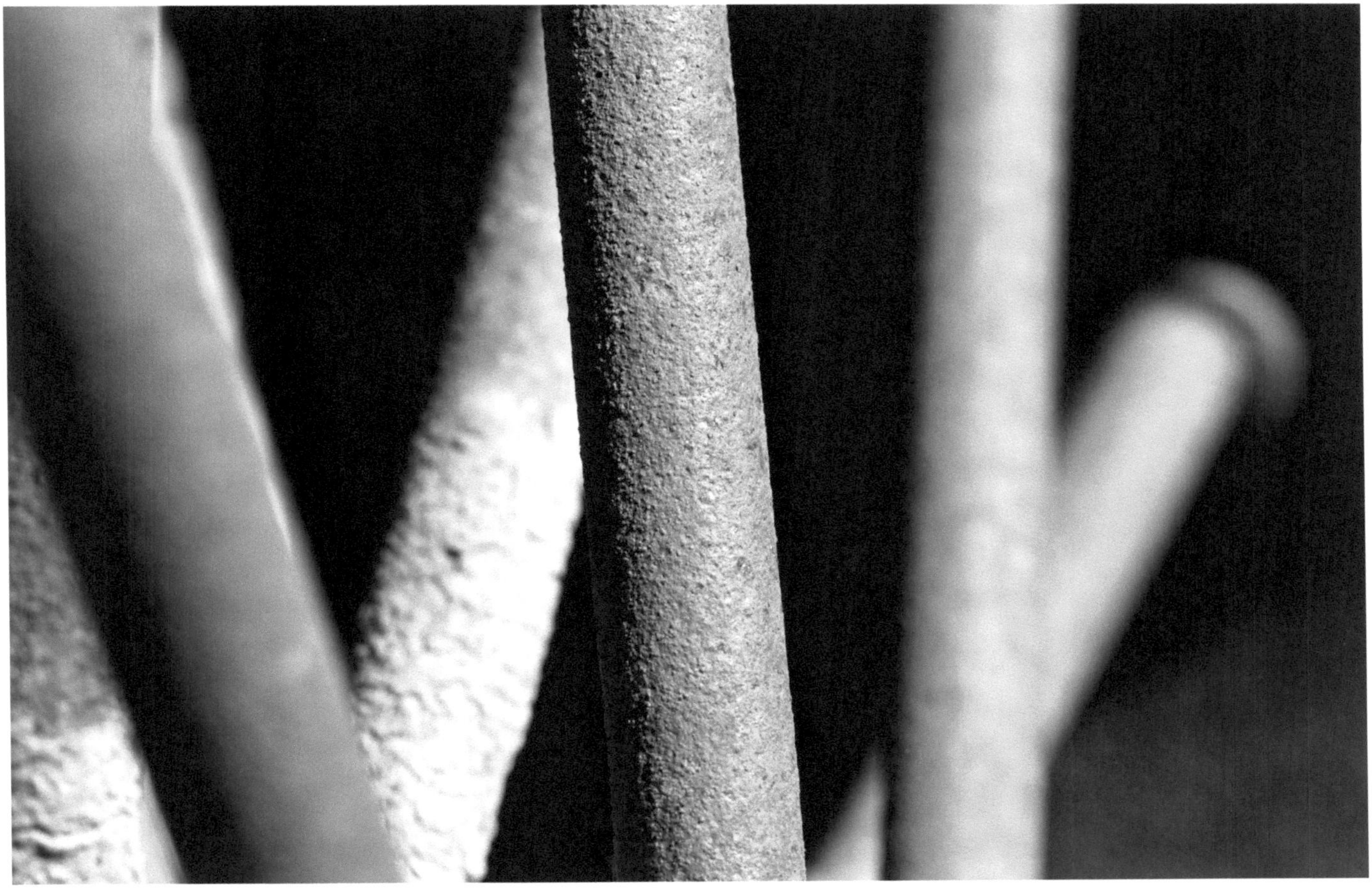
0780

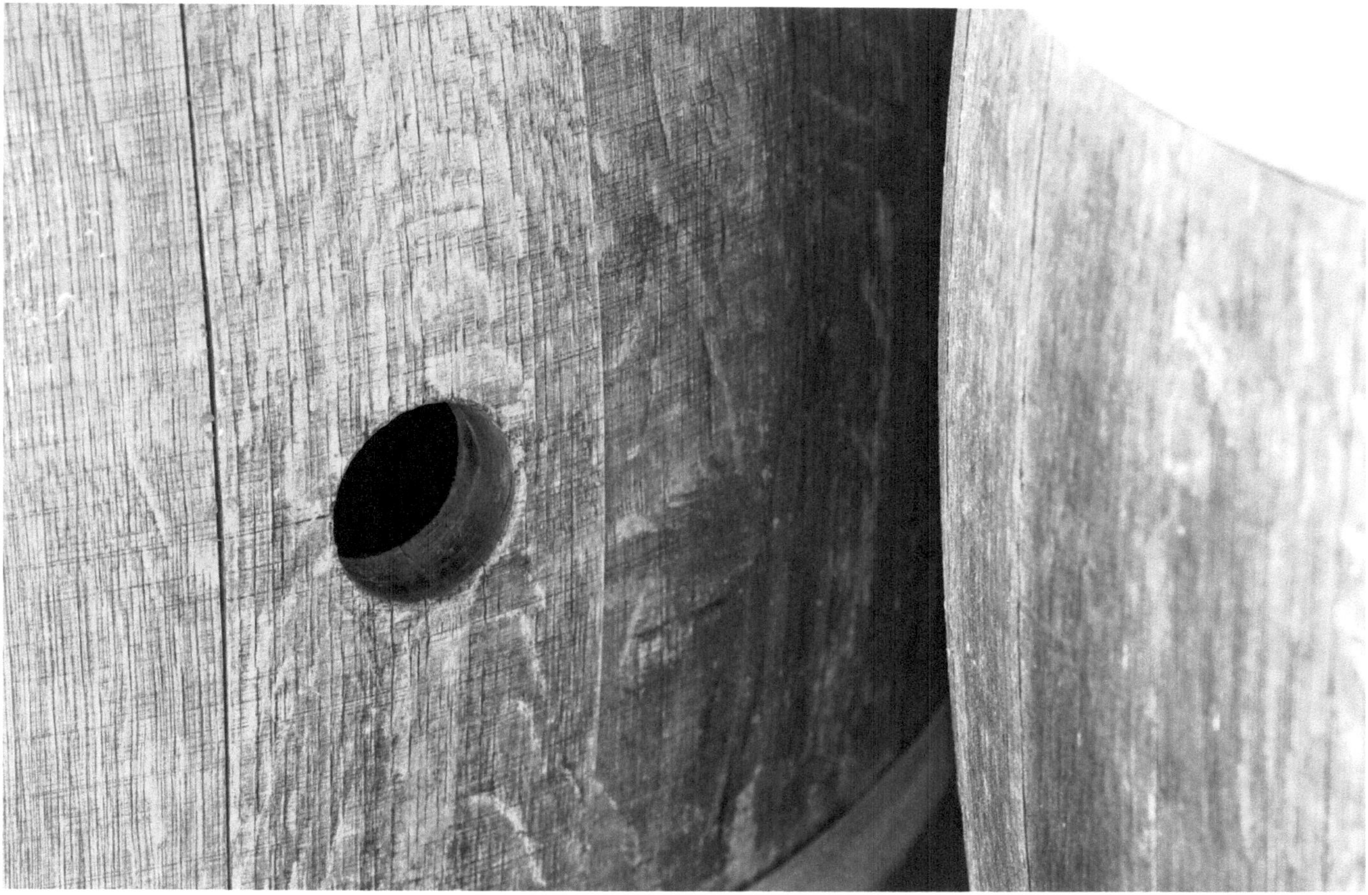
0826

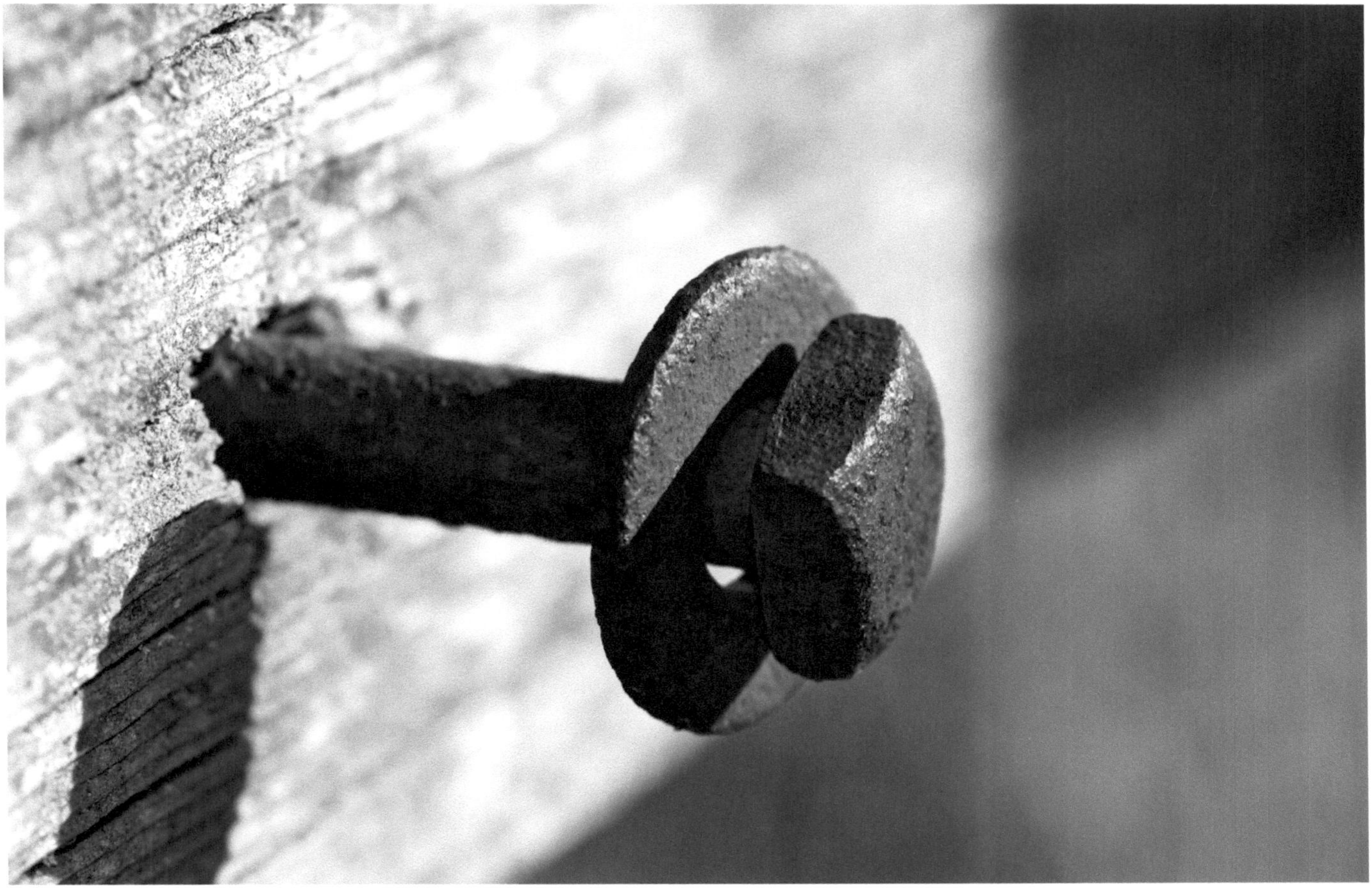

1173

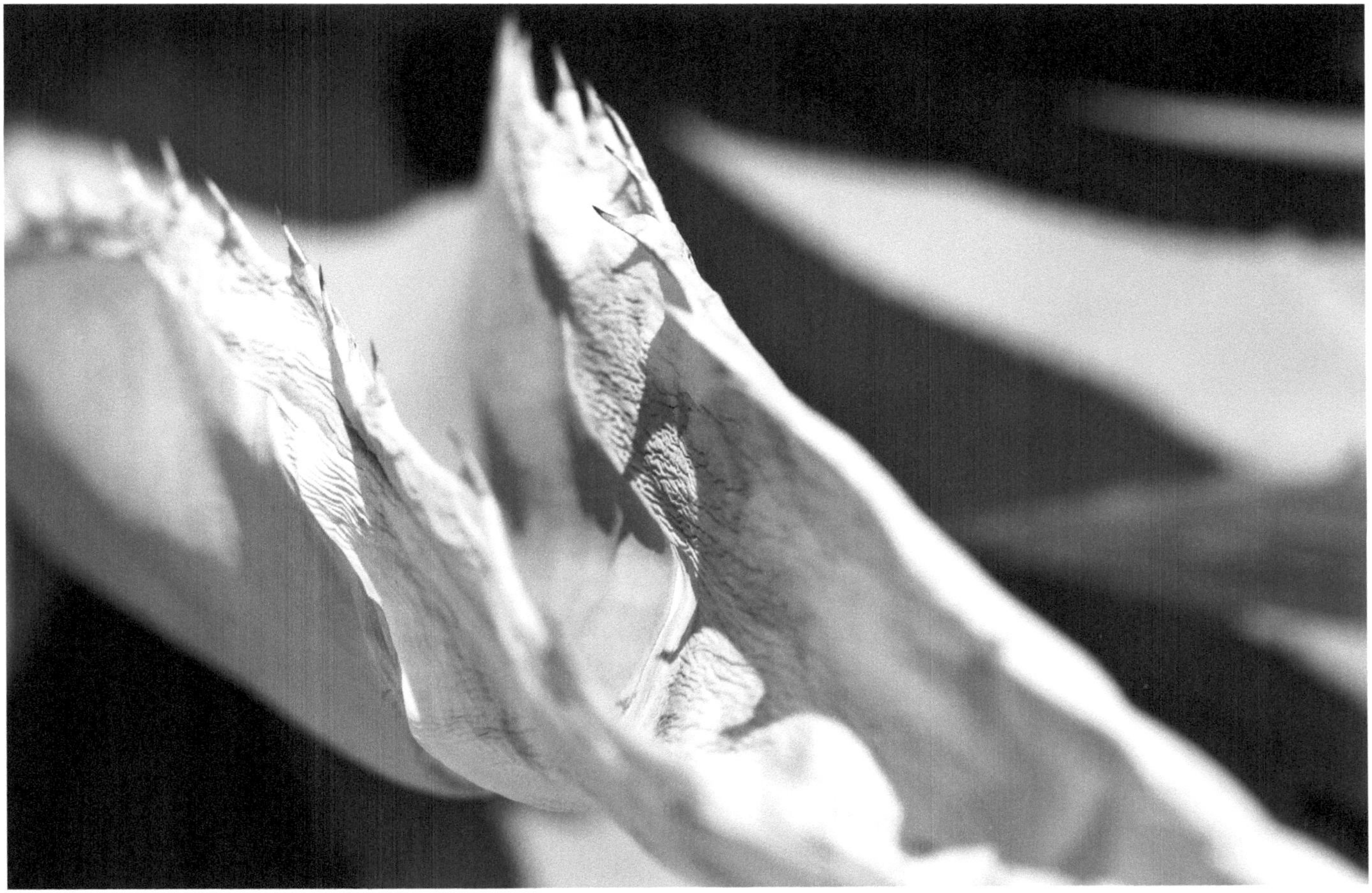
1581

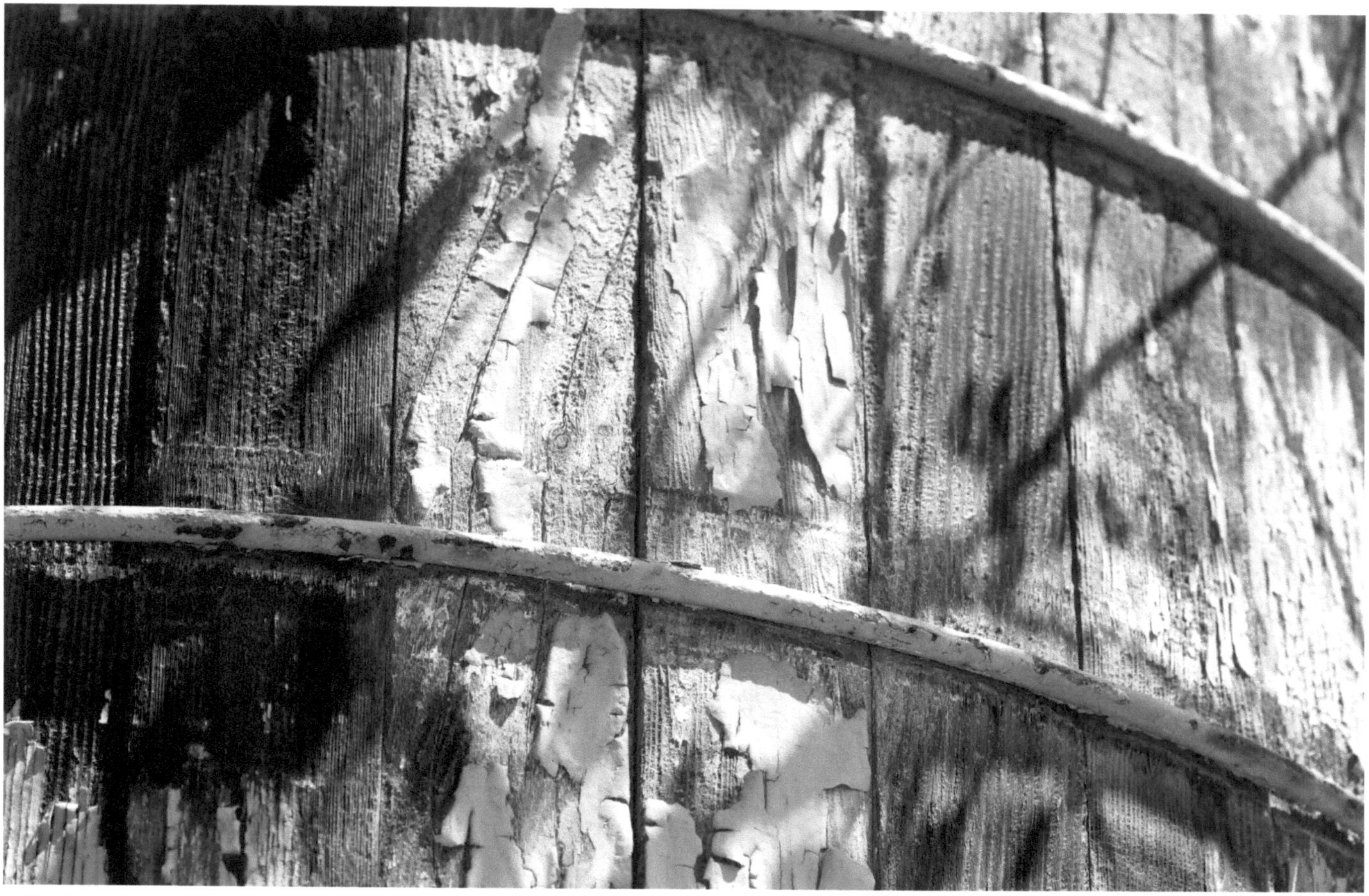

1608

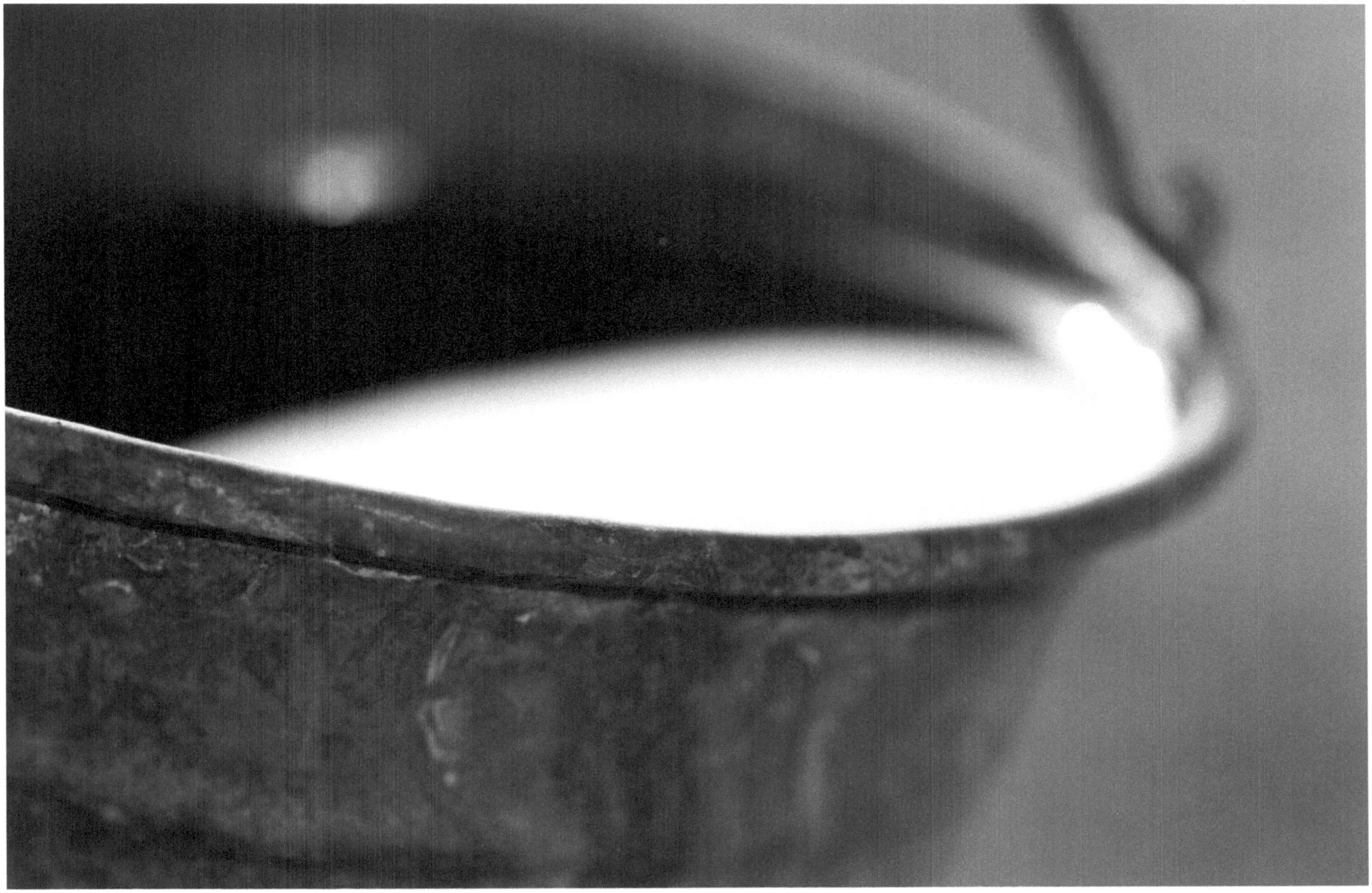

2180

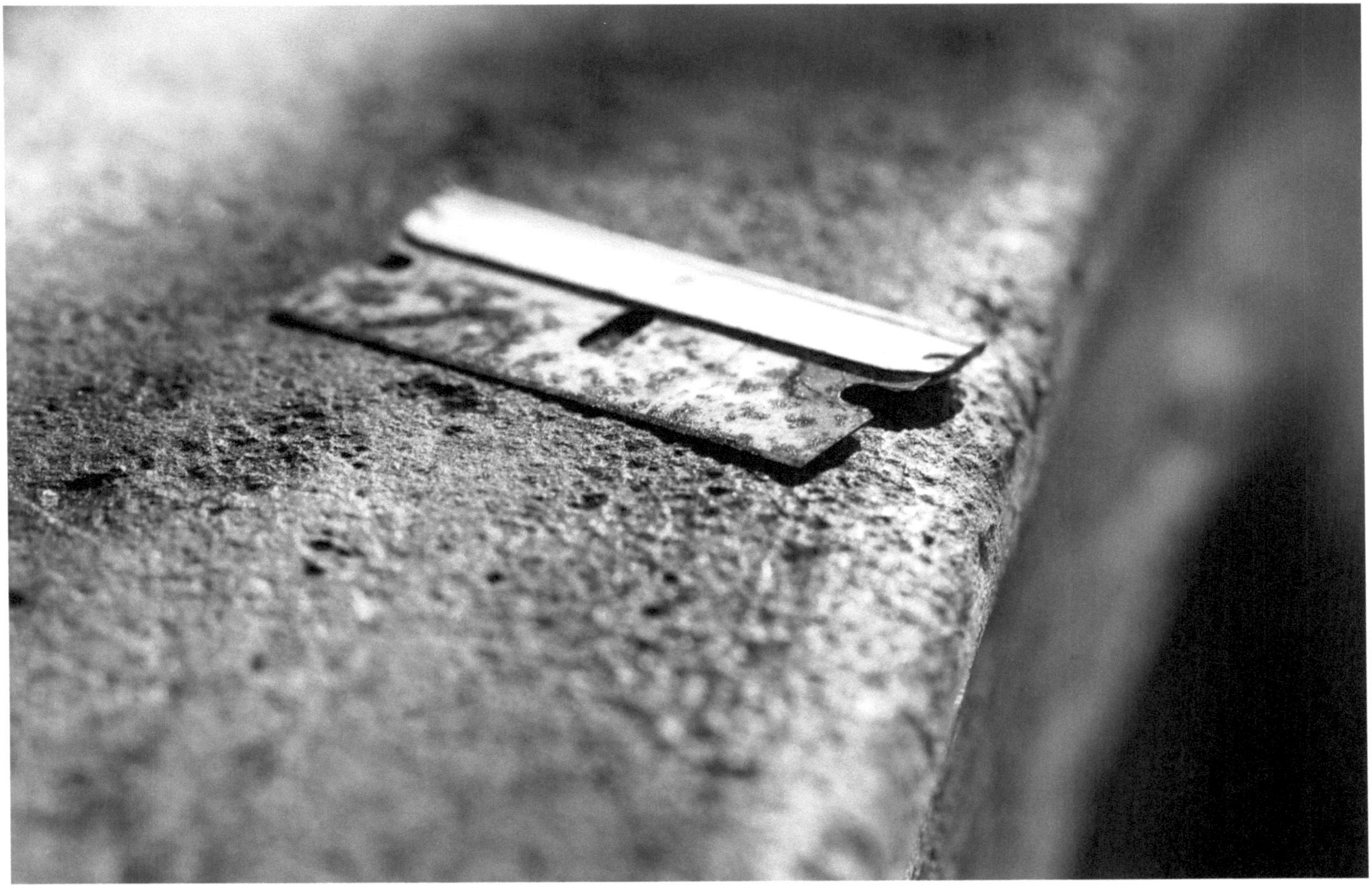

2467

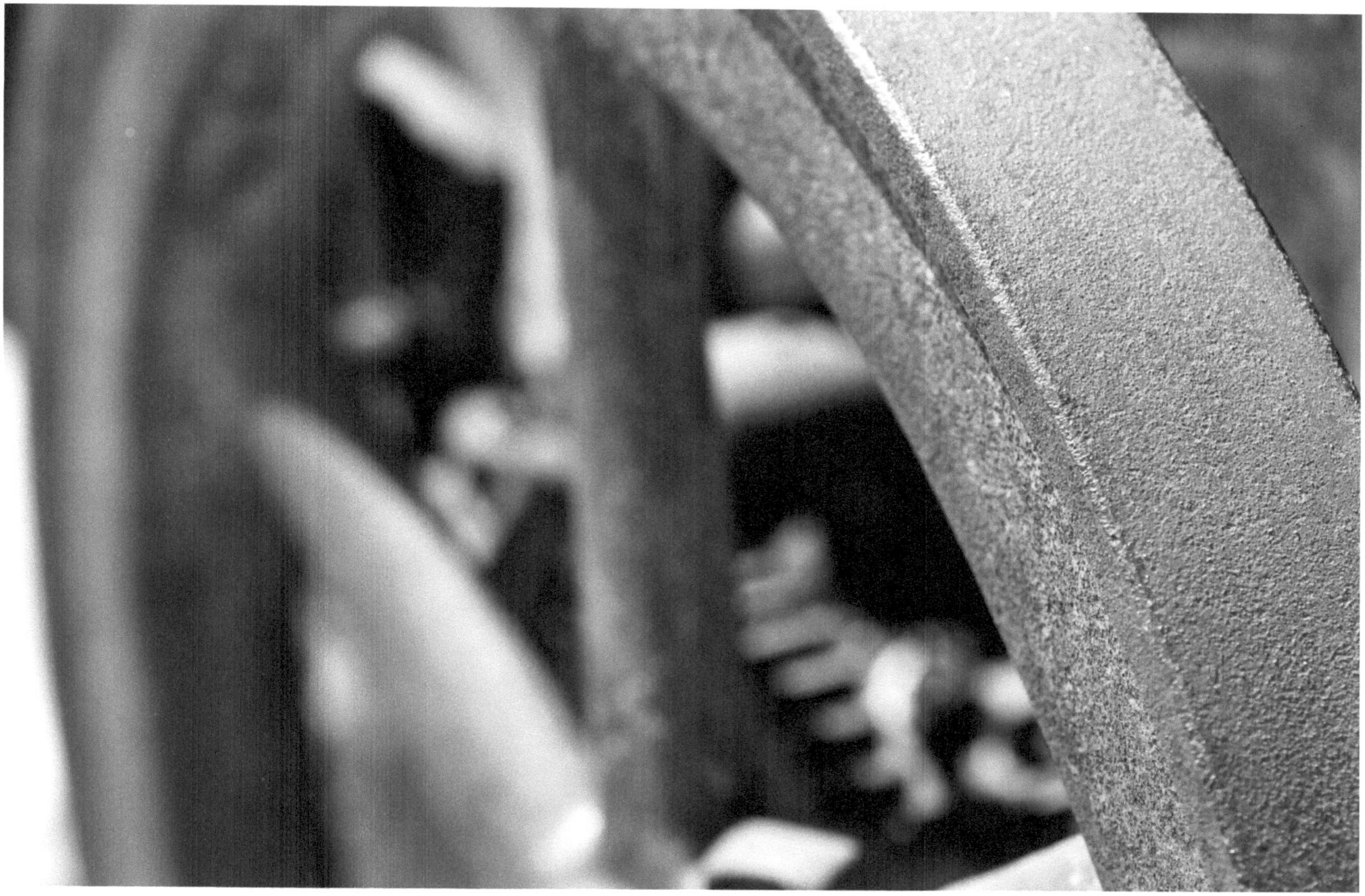

2962

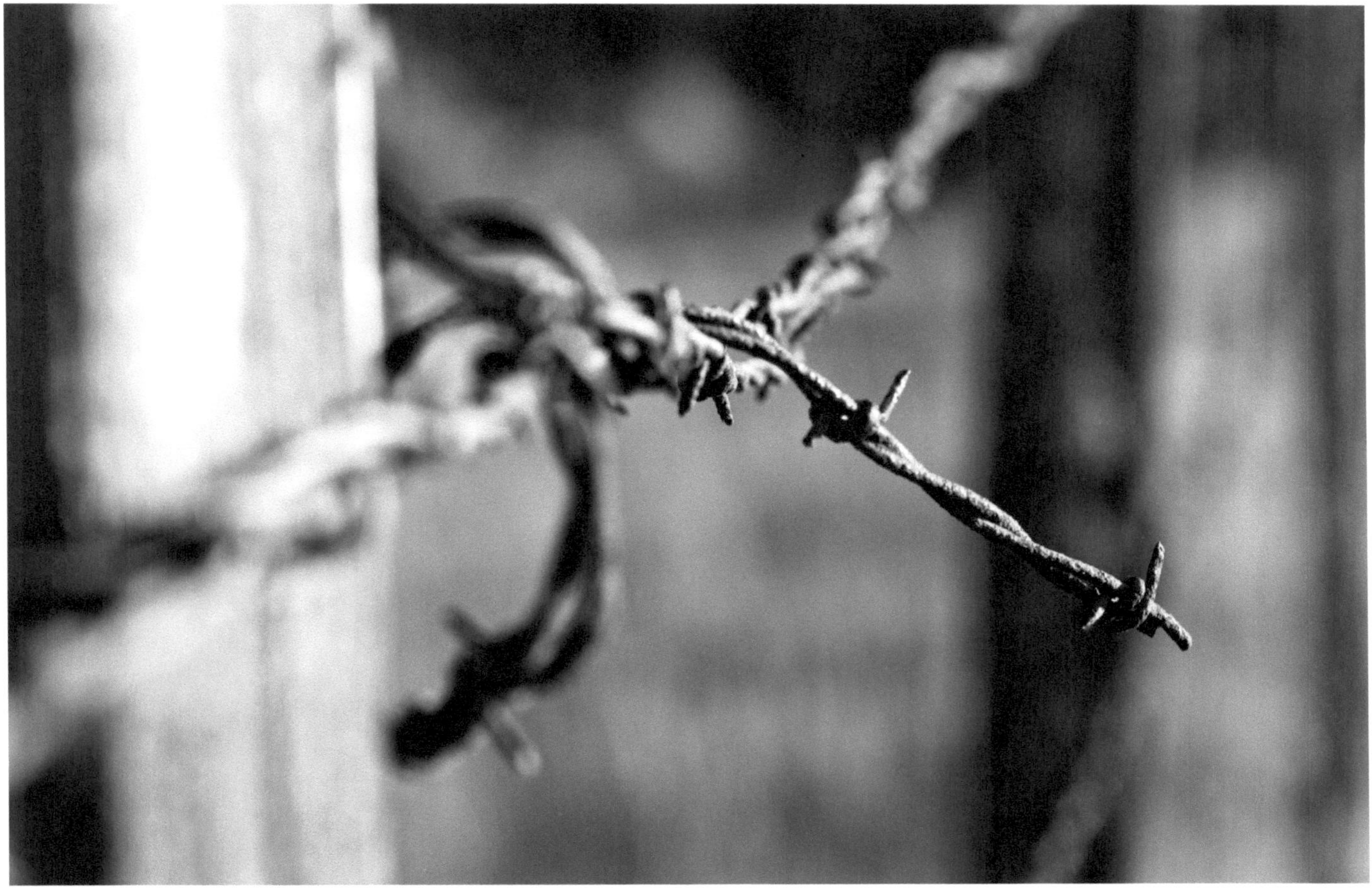

3359

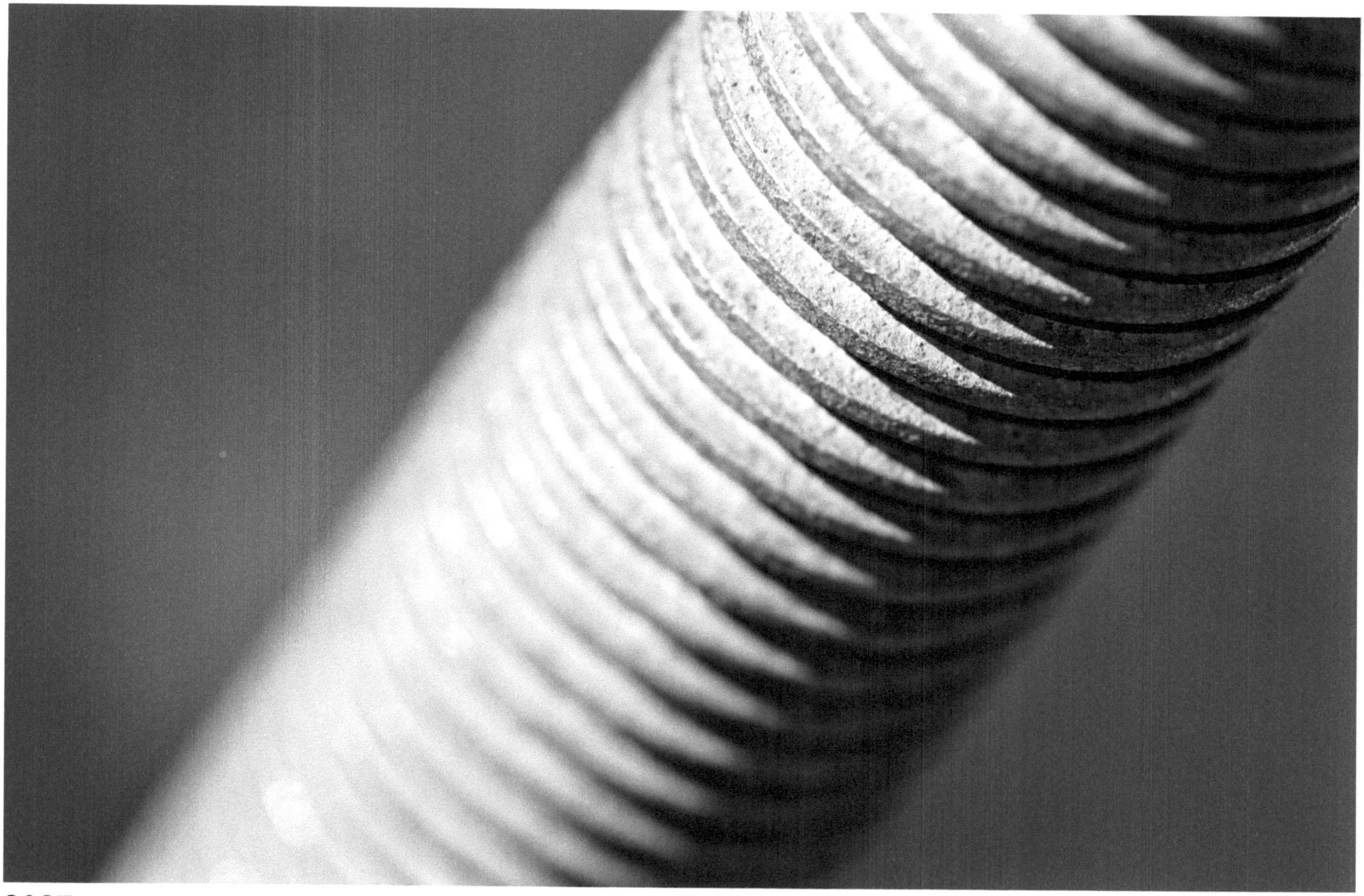

3937

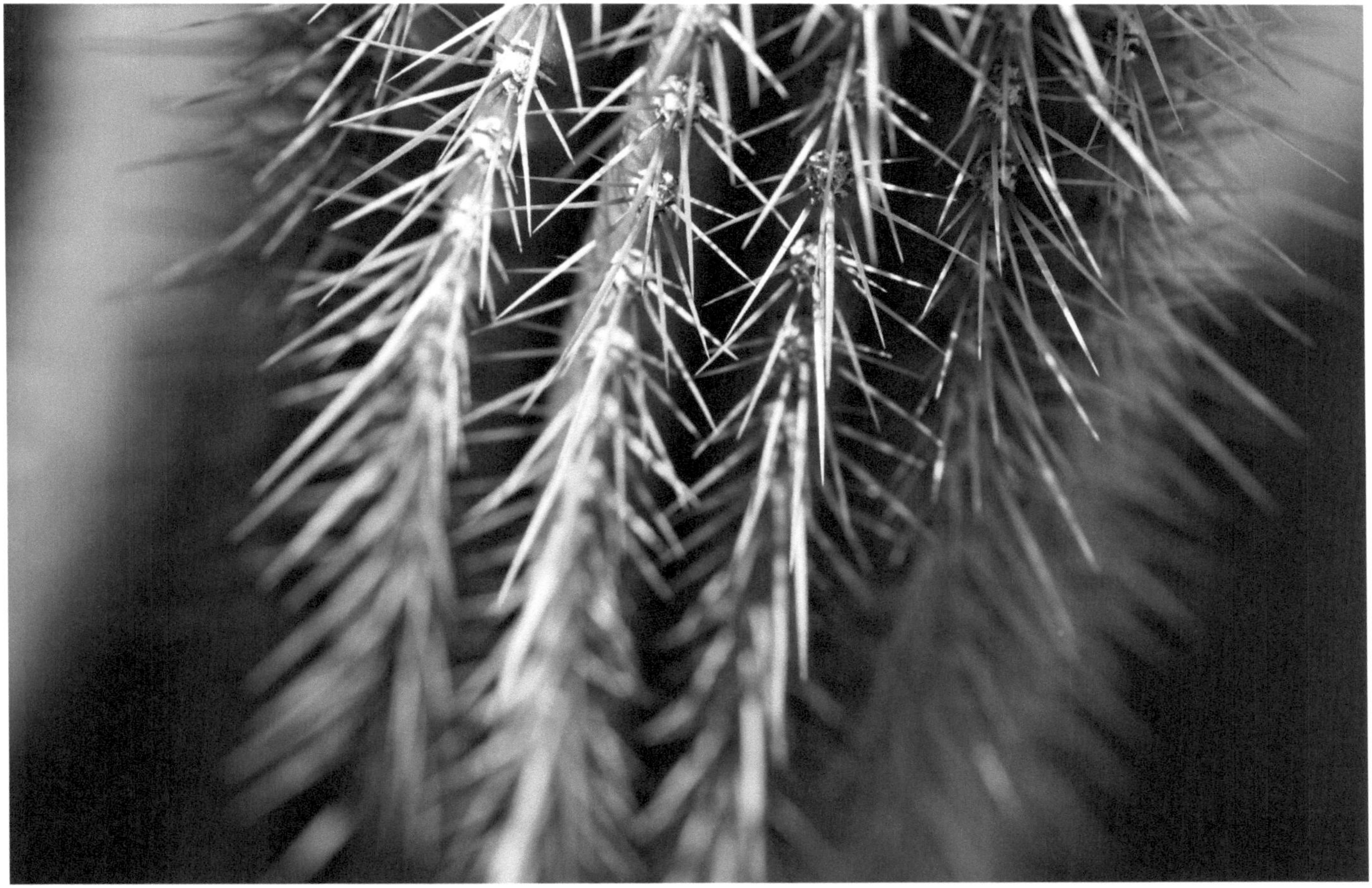

4070

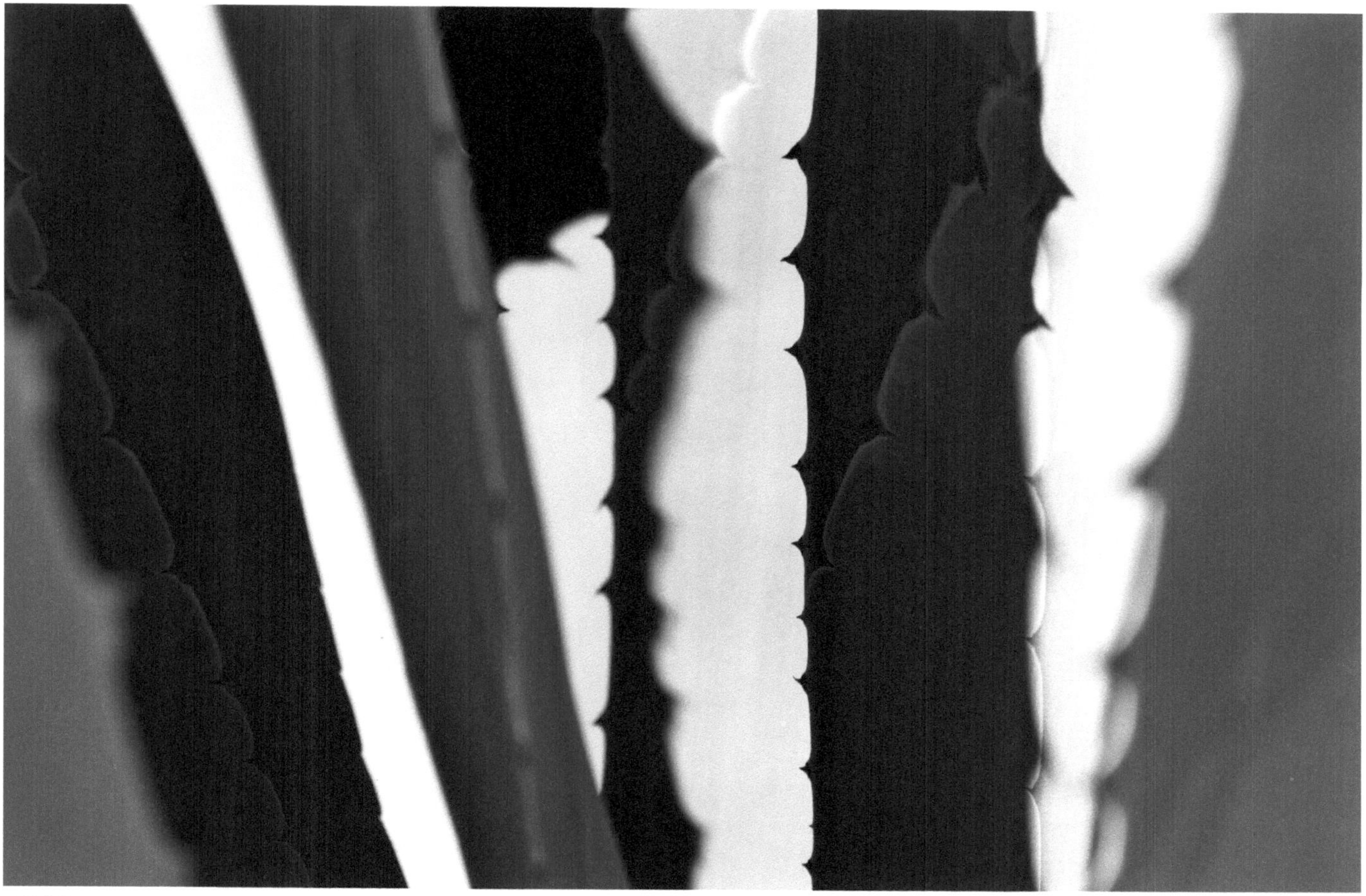

4099

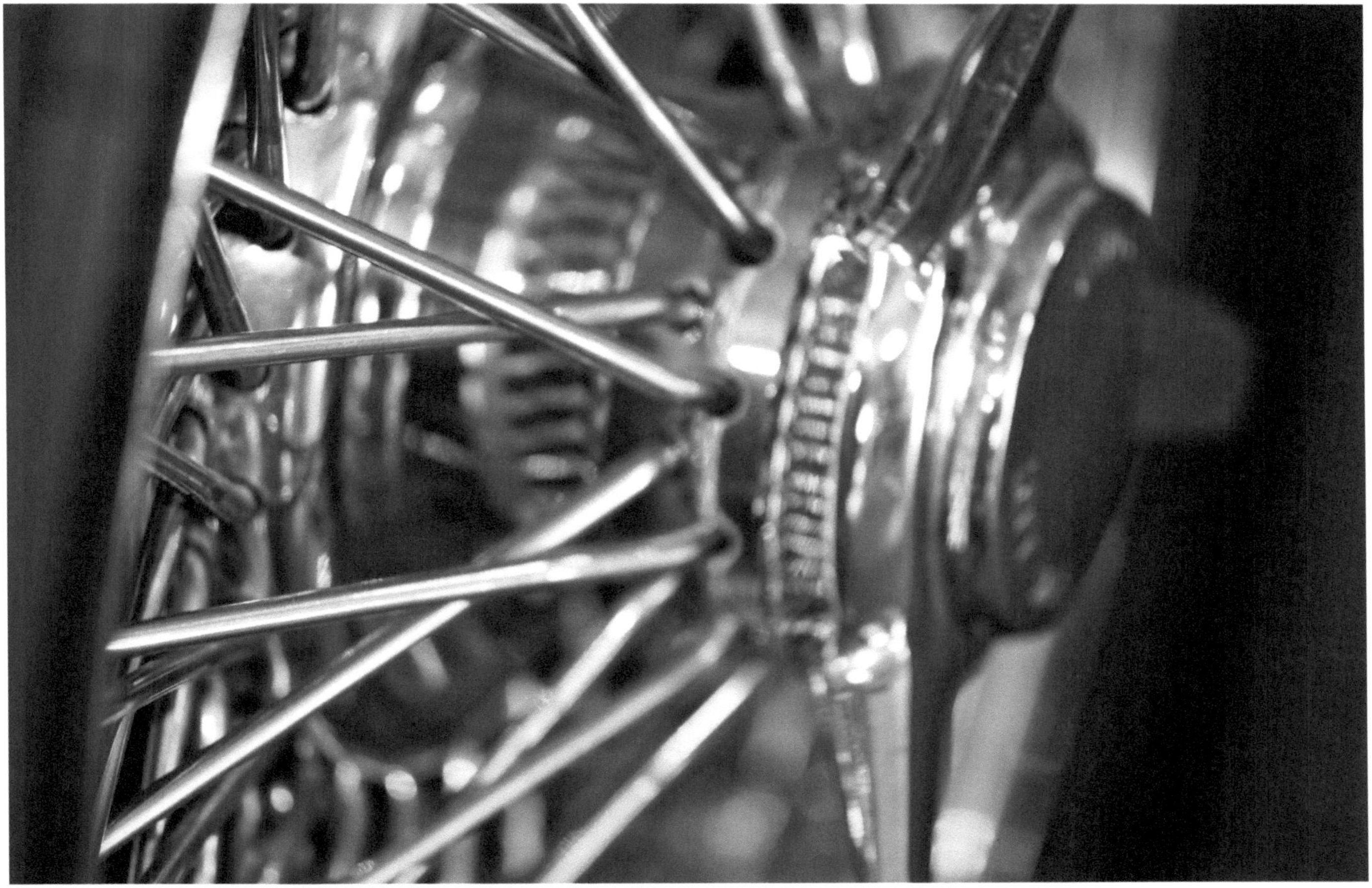

4193

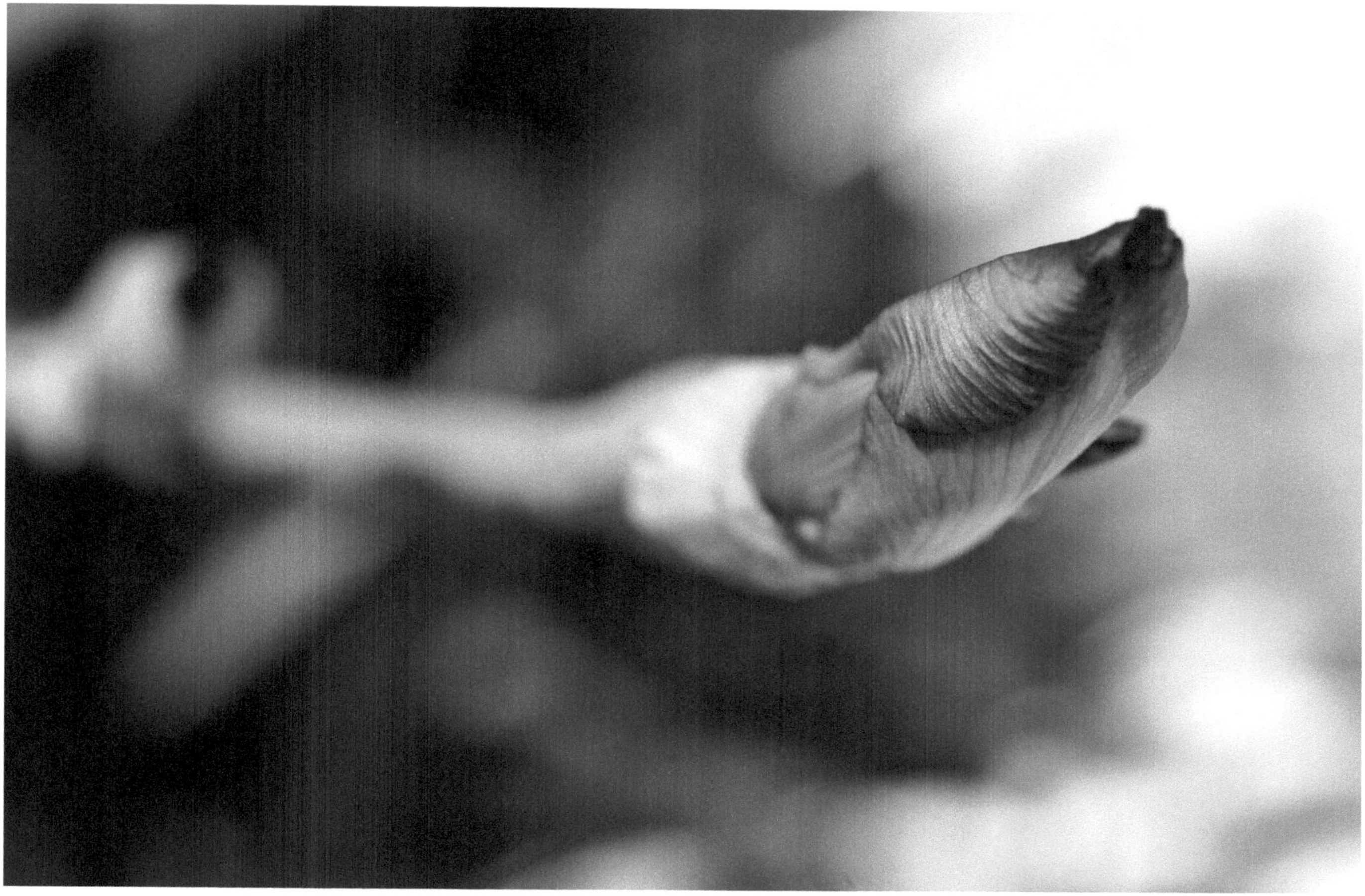

5492

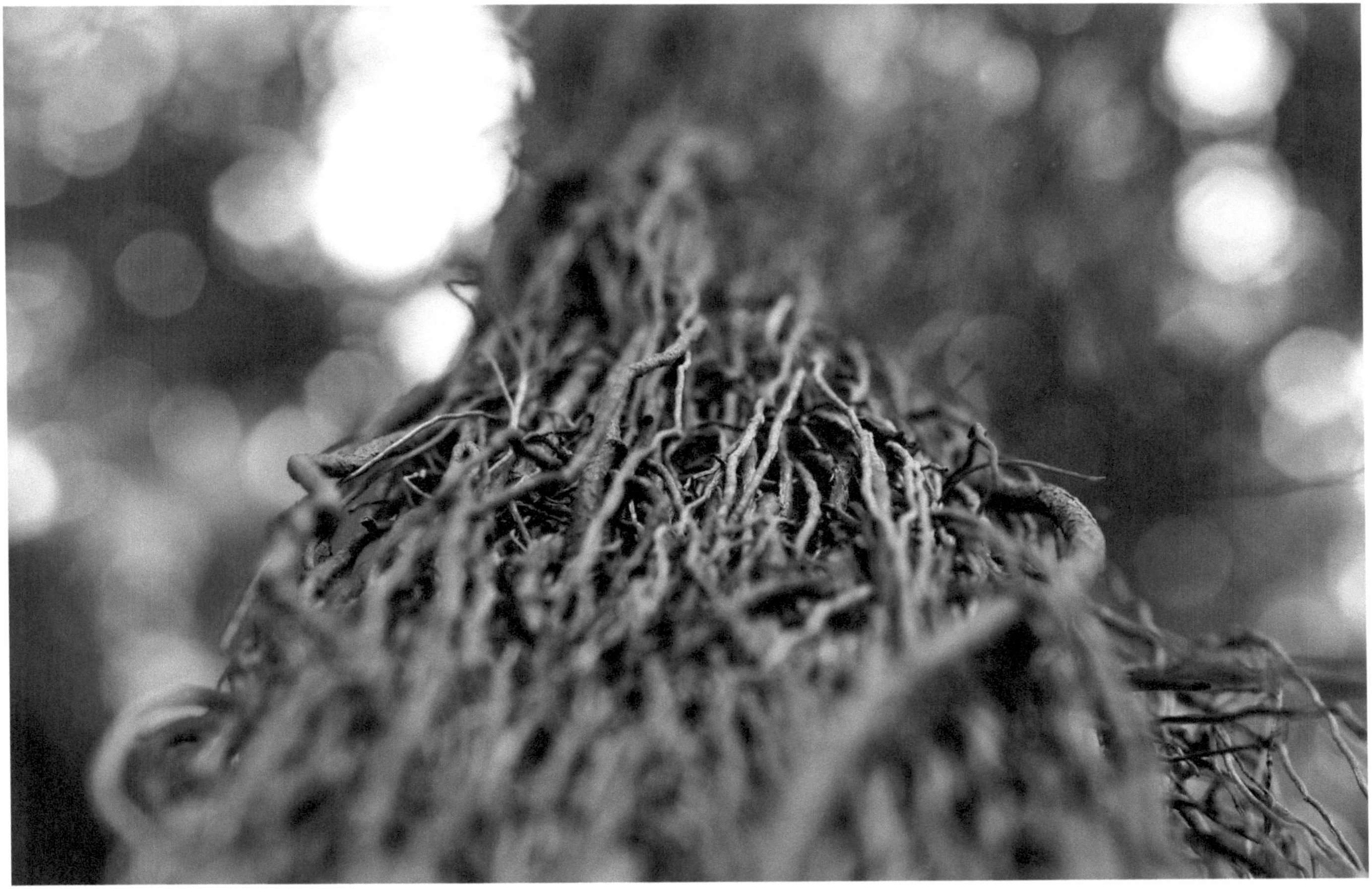

5811

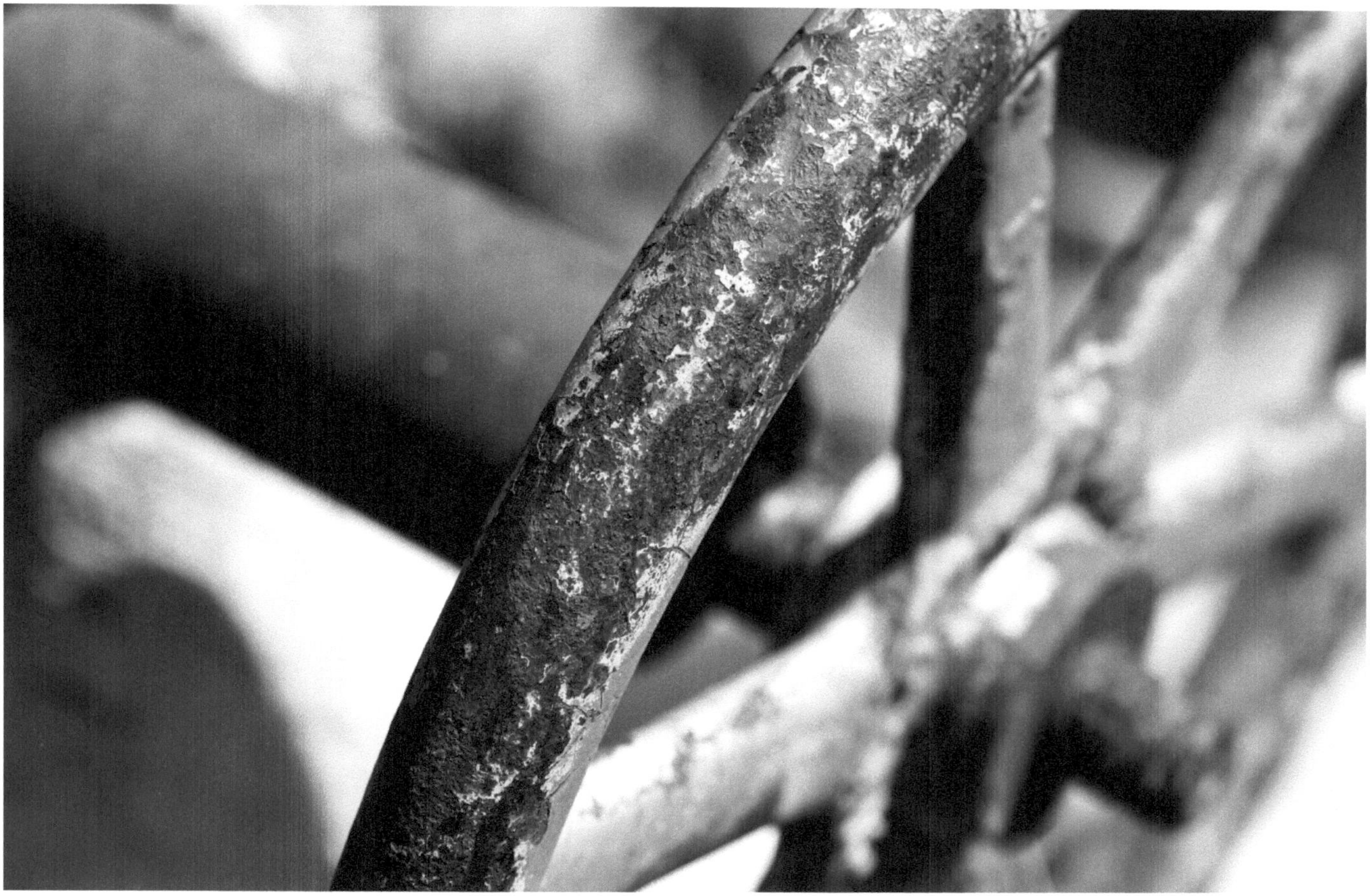
6095

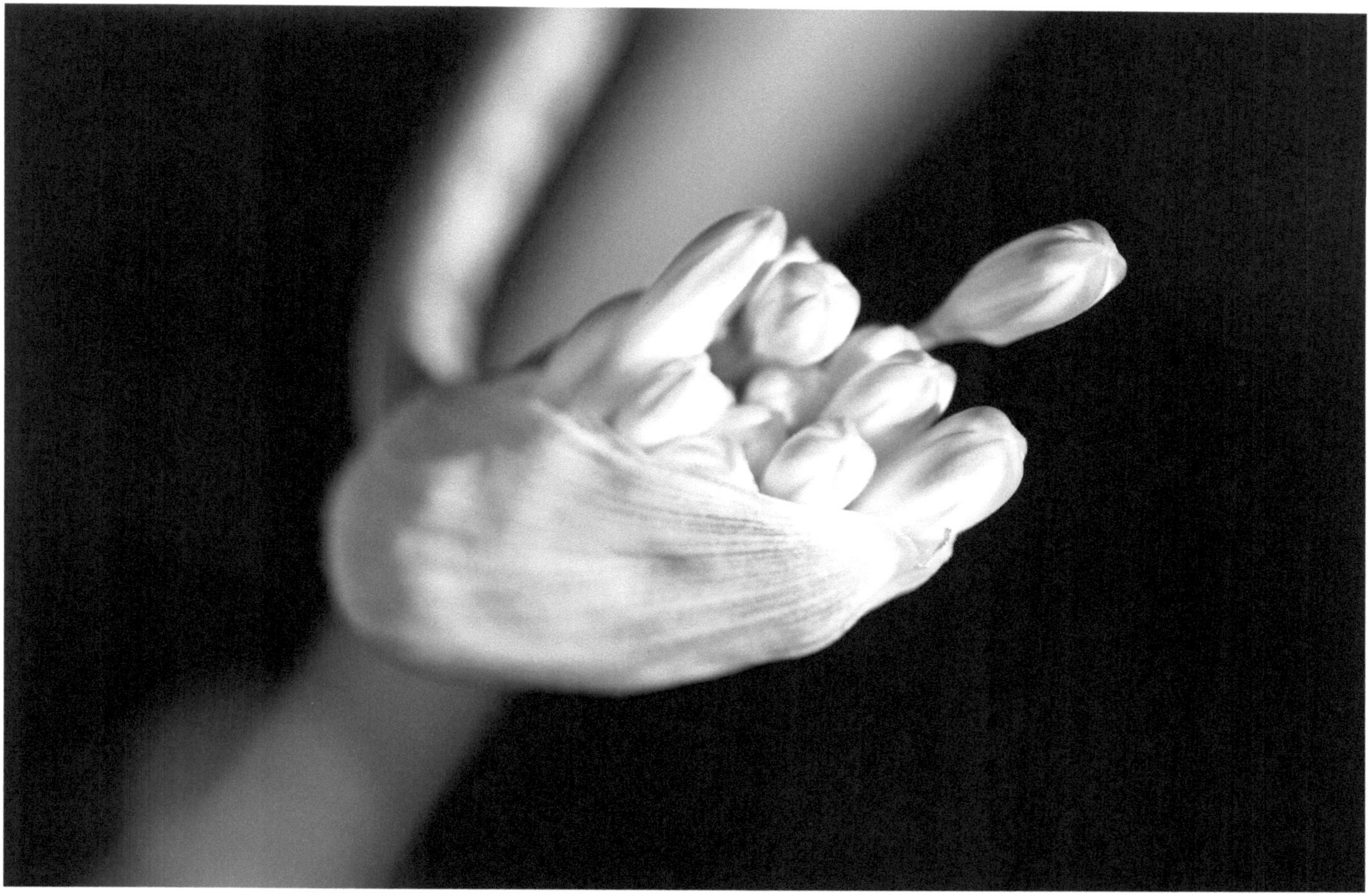

8407

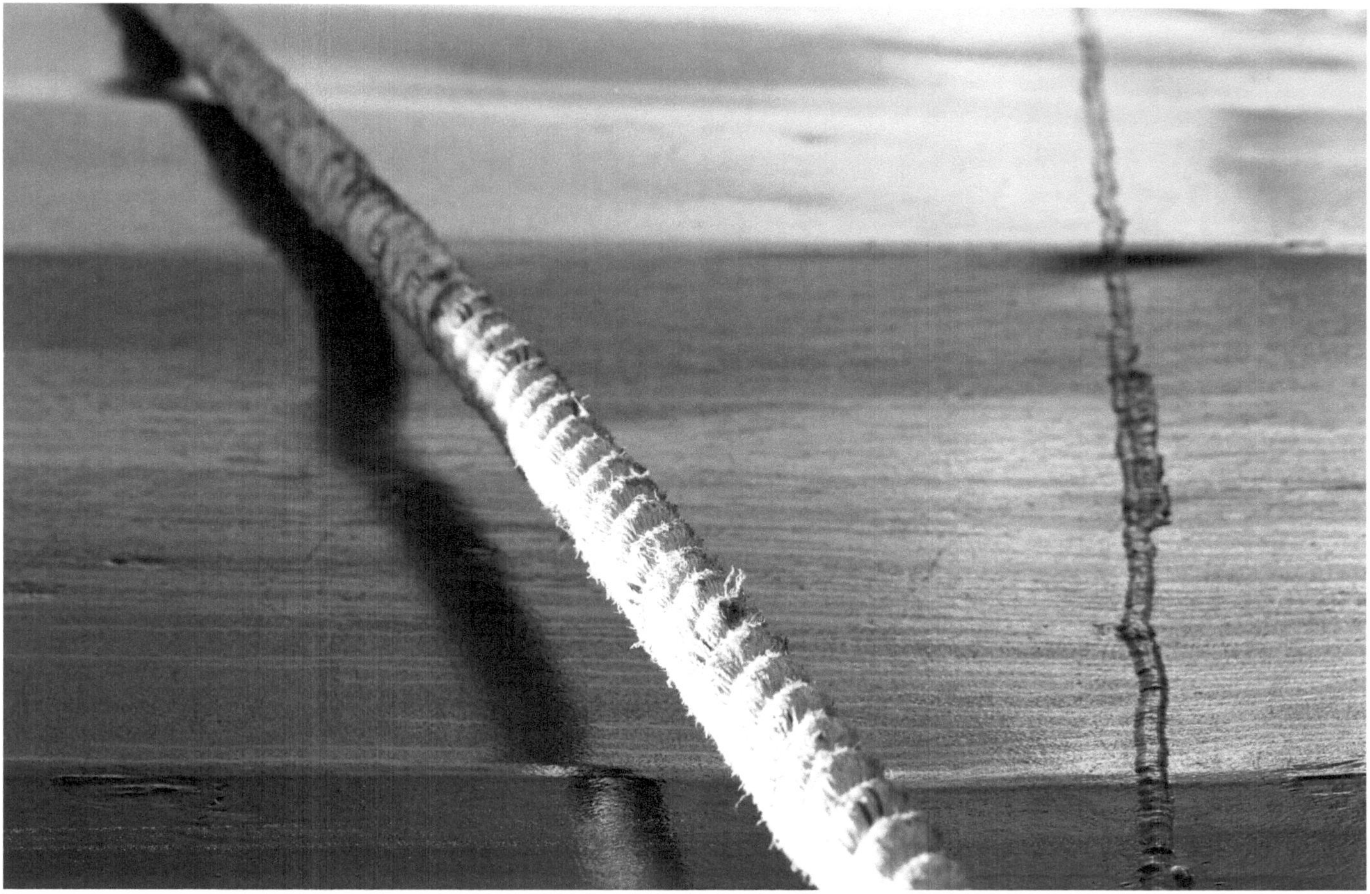

8470

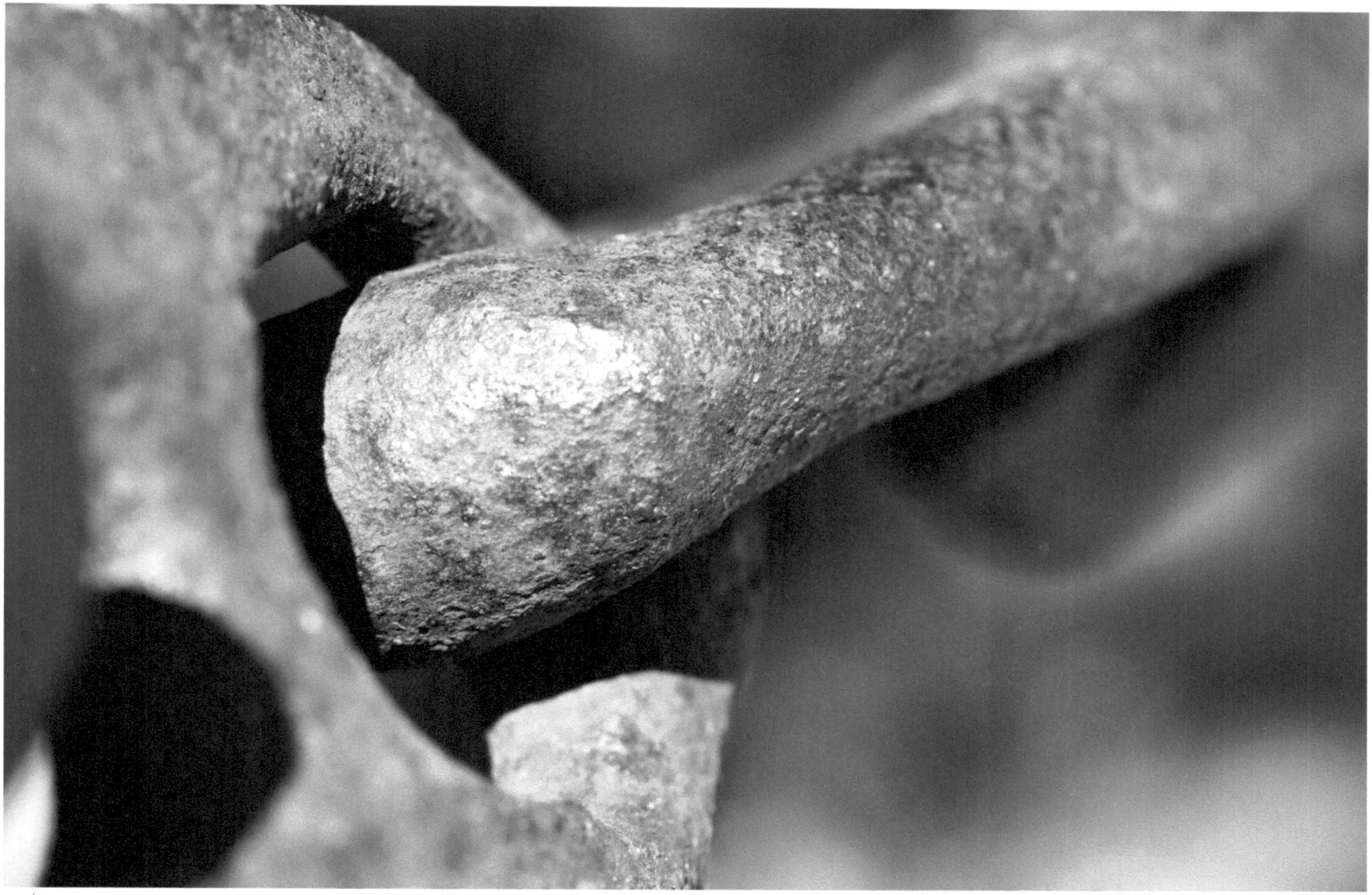

9353

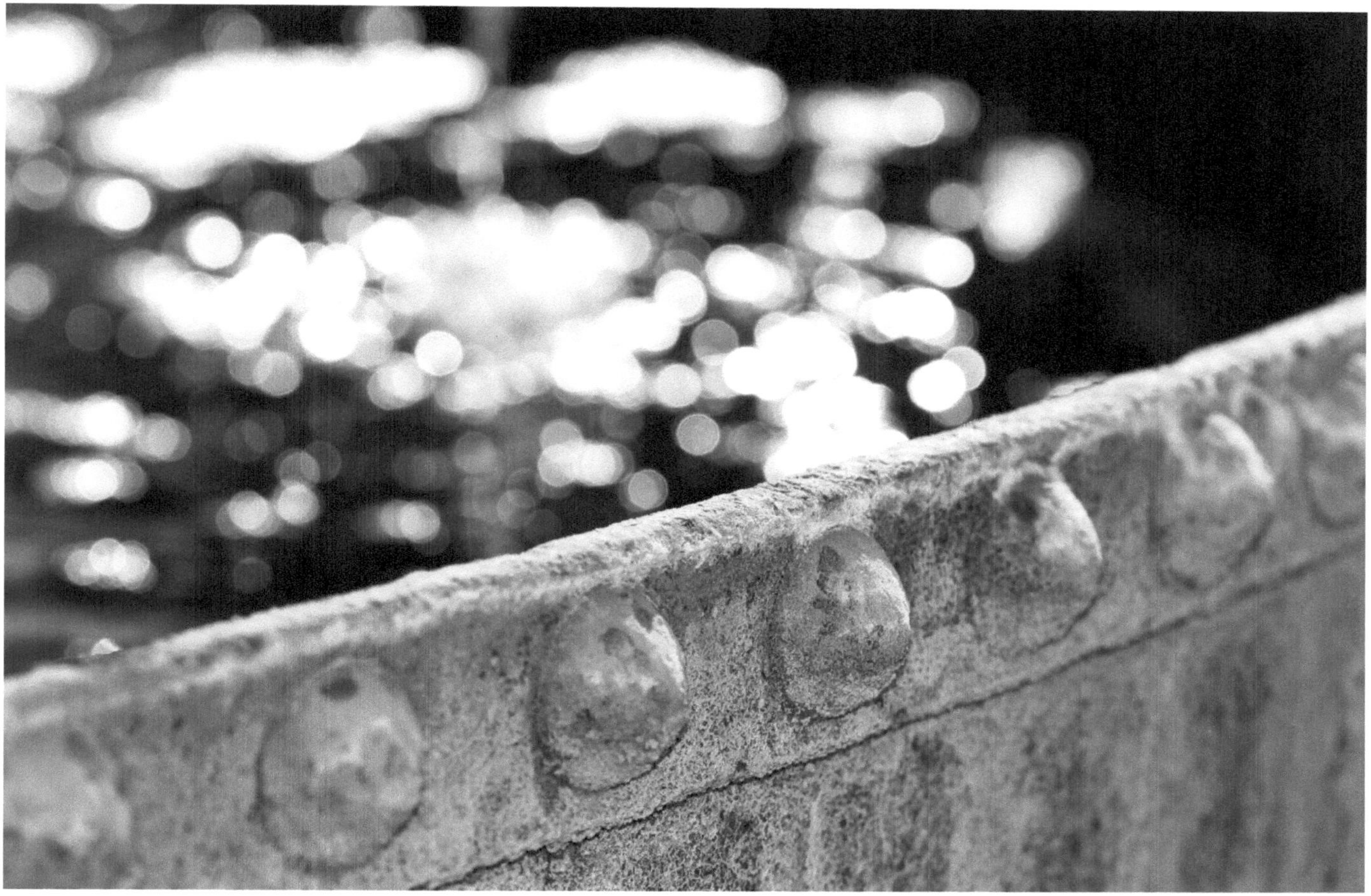
9430

www.ingramcontent.com/pod-product-compliance
Lightning Source LLC
Chambersburg PA
CBHW050836180526
45159CB00004B/1926
9781514834794